Tattle Tails

MARLENE FEKETE

NEWMAN SPRINGS PUBLISHING
320 Broad Street
Red Bank, NJ 07701

First originally published by Newman Springs Publishing 2023

ISBN 979-8-88763-226-1 (Paperback)
ISBN 979-8-88763-227-8 (Digital)

Printed in the United States of America

First and foremost, to my Savior, Jesus Christ, for opportunities to share my faith. Secondly, to my family and friends who have given me support. Also, to Newman Springs Publishing for seeing something and making it possible. Last but not least are all the furry animal friends who gave love and a listening ear and whom we hope to see in heaven, where rewards abound!

Contents

Introduction to Journal's Journey of Tattle Tails

Day 1 of Marlene's providential life: She was born with the middle name Frances, named after Saint Frances, the patron saint of animals. The book of Genesis tells the story of Jacob, who wanted to specialize in spotted black-and-white sheep and goats of both quality and quantity. With Marlene pursuing a similar specialty, a fate for Marlene followed. As life continued, she had six children but stopped due to a health issue. This led to a providential adoption of eleven severe and nonverbal special-needs children. She needed to learn a new language with nonverbal ways of communication! This led to another nonverbal life for her, raising as Jacob did, specializing in spotted black-and-white poodles. Balancing out her interest in fuzzy, furry friends came Yorkshire terriers. She continued with her strength of communication, bordering on mental telepathy! This journey will end, but who knows how Marlene Frances will say "amen."

Animals in the Beginning, Animals in the End!

From the wishing well, past the rainbow bridge, to the beginning of the heavenly traveled trip into heaven! As a dog breeder of twenty-five years, so many have called and shared their sorrow and the loss of their pet. They come wishing for more time or length of days. With a heavy heart and many tears, I write.

It has been a great reward as a Christian. I've had lifelong experience meeting people with pets. Sharing with them and caring for them has been a great reward, along with meeting Christians and nonbelievers alike in sharing my faith in God's creativity of each creature. This providence has brought about circumstances like placing God's little creatures into the hands of children with cancer in the Make-A-Wish Foundation and seeing them thrive beyond their time. The providence of God and all His timing and placement have been gratifying in terms of God's love and blessing in my life. I've seen God's hand move in the life of each circumstance and situation of each animal and how God reveals Himself in the love of all. And so I hope to write about the many ways that God has loved the world of mankind and animals.

Animals, Obedience, and God's Loving Care

The Bible tells us,

> Are not five sparrows sold for two farthings, and not one of them is forgotten before God? (Luke 12:6)

> And immediately the angel of the Lord smote him, because he gave not God the glory: and he was eaten of worms, and gave up the ghost. (Acts 12:23)

> Then began he to curse and to swear, saying, I know not the man. And immediately the cock crew. (Matthew 26:74)

> And the Lord spake unto the fish, and it vomited out Jonah upon the dry land. (Jonah 2:10)

God loves and cares for all animals, and they show Him their obedience in return. In obedience, creatures of God truly obey the voice of God, and faster than man!

> And the locust went up over all the land of Egypt, and rested in all the coasts of Egypt: very grievous were they; before them there were no such locusts as they, neither after them shall be such. (Exodus 10:14)

2

A locust swarm can contain over a trillion locusts, all listening to God's call! They were the army of God and still are the army of God every several years. The sound of the mighty wings is a sound to be reckoned with!

> For that which befalleth the sons of men befalleth beasts; even one thing befalleth them: as the one dieth, so dieth the other; yea, they have all one breath; so that a man hath no preeminence above a beast: for all is vanity. All go unto one place; all are of the dust, and all turn to dust again. (Ecclesiastes 3:19–20)

It may seem that all have one breath so that a man has no preeminence above the beast, that we all share the same lot in life, that we all go to one place, that we all are of the dust, and that we all turn to dust again. But I believe man will face judgment. The result of this judgment is either heaven or hell. Heaven is where God lives, and hell was created for Satan and his fallen angels. So where do animals go? Heaven, hell, or simply to dust? I do not believe the Bible speaks of animal judgment because animals are perfect in their obedience. Some believe that animals remain and are called to obey and stay on the earth while we go on after judgment.

I believe animals will be in heaven, along with our pets. God sent Noah to care for all animals so they could continue living with mankind thereafter. In the ark, animals were called, and the animals obeyed. I am sure Noah and his family loved those animals as much as the Lord did in calling them to come aboard the ark. We will still have animals in heaven. Where will those animals come from? When Jesus was asked about marriage, He made it clear that there would be no marriage in heaven: "For in the resurrection they neither marry, nor are given in marriage, but are as the angels of God in heaven" (Matthew 22:30). Does this mean no reproduction? What about reproduction in animals? If there is no animal reproduction, where will those animals come from? God will call animals upward, and they will obey Him. They are waiting in the dust patiently and will be obedient to his calling!

3

God, the User of Animals

Again in Jonah, we find several needed happenings where the Lord used animals. In Jonah chapter 4, we find God using the fish to swallow and spew Jonah out of its mouth. And a little further in the story, when dealing with Jonah in his anger, the Lord used the help of a bush and a worm. While the Bible speaks of Nineveh's rescue, He talks about the loss of one hundred thousand people and children, but also includes the loss of their cattle, again showing God's care and love. How can we not believe that our animals and pets are going to be every bit a part of God's paradise! Truly, Psalm 148 declares that every living thing made upon earth shall give praise, honor, and worship to the Lord. Our future home surpasses any human understanding. We do not know what awaits us in heaven. Scripture reveals that no eye has seen and no ear has heard; no one knows what is prepared for us and those who love him!

> But as it is written, Eye hath not seen, nor ear heard, neither have entered into the heart of man, the things which God hath prepared for them that love him. (1 Corinthians 2:9)

We can only imagine how wonderful the garden of Eden must have been and what an emotional loss it must have been for Adam and Eve to separate from God because of their disobedience. The pain of loss must have been horrific, going from walking with God to entering life without Him and making a way of life with the struggles of sin always before them. How so it was with all creation that had to struggle with the consequences. Everything in life became a separation! Being the final separation to death. God, in His mercy and through the cross, made a way to restore the separation. God sent his Son to restore eternal life for us to be able to regain the kingdom back with obedience back to repentance of our sins.

The Restoration of Eden, Earth, and Heaven

In the beginning, all things were created from *A* to *Z* and from Adam to zebra by God.

> For by him were all things created, that are in heaven, and that are in earth, visible and invisible, whether they be thrones, or dominions, or principalities, or powers: all things were created by him, and for him. (Colossians 1:16)

Adam was given the rule over animals in the garden of Eden. God gave Adam instructions to name all the animals. (I honestly would have loved it, but I cannot comprehend all those animals and naming them, pronouncing them, and then remembering all of them.) God did bring the animals and all living things to be named by Adam, but maybe it looked like it was too big a task for Adam alone, so He made Eve to help him.

Besides the land animals, it was also Adam's job to name all living things, which included things in the air and in the sea. God also gave Adam the job of ruling over them and caring for them. Adam had a gigantic job. The Lord commanded Adam to care for them, and even up to today, we care for the animals, including our pets!

For this reason, I think our own pets will be there when we are called to go! We are told animals will be there; we are told the lion will lie down together with the lamb. What kind of love can there be that does not envision pets joining us? How did they get there, and where did they come from? God is creating a new heaven and a new earth—not new humans, as He made us for eternity, and not new animals, as God already made them. What's left to envision God creating? Maybe the plan is to reunite man and animal! From God's goodness, God has promised to wipe away our tears! Could this be from our separation of losing our pets and loved ones? When we come together after the separation, we go into a new beginning where tears are wiped away. It is most probable and logical to believe that pets will come along in song and worship, rejoicing in the Lord for His goodness and love for all His creation. God's creation makes perfect sense for harmony and balance to keep His creation ever present for His glory and worship! Scripture speaks of the lion that will lie down with the lamb—not just our beloved pets, but the love of God's whole creation and goodness, never speaking of any more loss. Believe the love you shared will be shared, though in a greater dimension than we can perceive, knowing it is all for God's glory, worship, and praise! God's creation speaks of only love and continuation; the rest will remain a mystery till we meet again.

The Sound of Music of
a Different Tune

I believe that when we all get together, the sounds of all will be in heaven, whether animal or human. I picture it all as music to our ears. The reason I believe this is because at the time of the Tower of Babel, the language was universal to all, but because sin was there, the Lord gave them a new way to go and communicate. Each went their own way, having to form a new understanding and develop a new tongue to be understood. Well, as you can see up to today, that has failed miserably.

Sometimes, I can't understand what is going on around me, even in my own household! For that reason and personal experience, I believe that in heaven, all things pertaining to communication will be of a new mind, soul, and spirit. Perhaps mental telepathy might be that kind of communication! Unless the praise and worship of the Lord will be in a new tongue. After all, we will have a new name. Also, I think the old language, whatever that tongue was, will be universal to all as the one and only. This is the vision of my imagination, and I love the beauty of what could be! All creation sings.

Recently, while exploring the internet, I came across some technology that confirmed my thoughts and beliefs about music in plants. Plants play their own music! We cannot hear it without the technology, but how much more will we learn of God's wonderful orchestra now and in heaven! Animals will have their own musical tune. We will also have many sounds and tones. Everything, including us, will have its own sound and tone.

I perceive instruments of all kinds, including harps and horns, to play every different melody. Throughout the decades, every tone, melody, and note in every scale has been played or sung. From Jewish style to today's rock beat, even favorite old-time hymns (which I believe had a salvation message to them), yet nothing will compare to the heavenly sound anew when heaven comes our way.

I want to think that my era of music was derived from the Scripture and feel that it is the one most dear to the Lord's ear because of the Scripture and testimony of God's love. The salvation and the testimony to my faith came to my ears through "How Great Thou Art." With a little heaven in the soul, many songs have brought tears to our eyes. But I think it would be vanity to think the Lord would bring our earthly music into heaven! He has an orchestra of creation waiting for us to hear!

Chat Room of a Soul's Harbor

So let's talk to the animals.

> The beast of the field shall honour me, the drag-
> ons and the owls: because I give waters in the
> wilderness, and rivers in the desert, to give drink
> to my people, my chosen. (Isaiah 43:20)

Let's give honor where honor is due and proclaim even from the animals unto the Lord! Heaven, animals, and human beings bring the song to my heart: "When we all get to heaven, what a day of rejoicing that will be" ("When We All Get to Heaven" by E. E. Hewitt). What a wonderful worship that will be! Animals, us and our pets, not forgetting our lost loved ones whom, with providence and grace, God chose to include!

> And he said unto them, Go ye into all the world, and
> preach the gospel to every creature. (Mark 16:15)

Does this include animals? Heaven forbid! Excluding creatures from heaven is not scriptural, so as to be included as part of heaven. The word *creature* is presented as part of God's love and accepted as part of the plan in the Scriptures. Creatures do not need to be preached or witnessed to because God used animals for His glory. When man disobeyed God's animals, animals came through for Him, all for His glory. When disobedience came from man, creatures were the objects to bring repentance and forgiveness from varying sources to do God's bidding. But Jesus Christ alone brings forgive-ness and repentance to those who seek, search, and for those who find. Creatures will be just that: creatures of God's love, with no thought to being used as a means or tool to help in the quest of the will of God toward salvation or obedience.

Who Am I, Who Are You

We all fall short of the glory of God. I, for one, consider myself a scatterbrain at many times in my life and have fallen short in obedience to my given purpose in life. God can raise humans, animals, and even solid structures to bring about His will for His glory! In the mercy and love of God, the final finish brings us to salvation! Satan, in his misery, knows he is going to lose the battle of his act and art in a world that is doomed. He will lose this world, including humans and animals. Since the fall of mankind in the garden of Eden, he has owned the world. But that is coming to an end! Satan will not be the prince of air and ruler of the earth anymore; the more he knows he's losing, the more this world will wax worse for his trying! The battle of sin will die, as Christ covered the death on the cross for us, our sins. Forgiveness and the promise of a new eternal life will be given to us.

Who am I? I might be a friend from your past. Maybe you are my future friend. Something I can do so you can get to know me better is some light humor. I once read (author unknown), "To get maximum attention, you simply cannot beat a gigantic blunder!" Yes, that's pretty much who I am! My prayer is such that somehow a message will reach you, especially if you are a soul in need of salvation. In your search for that wishing well for your pet, perhaps your search is for Jesus Christ. May you reach the well of living water and those awaiting you.

Animal Redemption, Is There Such a Thing?

I can boldly say no. There is no animal redemption. Christ died for the sins of mankind, not for the sins of animals. Could this be because animals need no redemption? We will joyfully share a place in heaven. Scripture speaks of animals in heaven. Since there is no reproduction in heaven, then assuming these creatures, including pets, will follow. After our calling, where would the multitude of them come from? There seem to be ranks of order in angels, humans, animals, and plants. No matter what the rank of order, one thing I know for sure is that whether something is made in the image of Christ or not, all creation was made to worship the Lord. Animals do not have a conscience for redemption as humans, but they certainly have been given the ability to sense things—not right from wrong but an ability to sense deeper. To hear what we can't, to smell what we can't, to see beyond our sight, and maybe even to be used for God's glory far more than we could imagine.

Talk to the Animals and a Stone's Voice Thrown In

And he answered and said unto them, I tell you
that, if these should hold their peace, the stones
would immediately cry out. (Luke 19:40)

All I can say is "wow" and "amen!"

For the stone shall cry out of the wall, and the beam
out of the timber shall answer it. (Habakkuk 2:11)

Again, "amen!" Even the timbers are getting involved. It is so
amazing that the rocks, walls, and timbers respond! It seems that sin
was the cause since mankind chose to sin instead of glorify, bringing
the stones to cry and the timbers to respond!

The bird on the boat was used to help Noah and his family determine when it was ready to go on land. The dove showed
obedience to the call of God, revealing how we—as humans—can
relate to the call of God. We need to listen to the small voice of
obedience within!

Bird in the Air, Bird on the Boat, and Balaam's Error

Now I know where the saying "a little birdie told me" comes from.

> Curse not the king, no not in thy thought; and curse not the rich in thy bedchamber: for a bird of the air shall carry the voice, and that which hath wings shall tell the matter. (Ecclesiastes 10:20)

> And the donkey saw the angel of the Lord standing in the way, and his sword drawn in his hand: and the donkey turned aside out of the way, and went into the field: and Balaam smote the donkey, to turn her into the way. But the angel of the Lord stood in a path of the vineyards, a wall being on this side, and a wall on that side. And when the donkey saw the angel of the Lord, she thrust herself unto the wall, and crushed Balaam's foot against the wall: and he smote her again. And the angel of the Lord went further, and stood in a narrow place, where was no way to turn either to the right hand or to the left. And when the donkey saw the angel of the Lord, she fell down under Balaam: and Balaam's anger was kindled, and he smote the donkey with a staff. And the Lord opened the mouth of the donkey, and she said unto Balaam, What have I done unto thee,

that thou hast smitten me these three times?
(Numbers 22:23–28)

For every time disobedience happens, it seems the Lord will go to the animals and angels. This time Balaam's sin caused an angel to help Balaam's donkey! Balaam abused the pet he had for many years, abusing her by swatting her, and the angel of the Lord stepped in to rescue her, stopping her from getting injured anymore. Will Balaam have remorse when he sees her in heaven? I surely feel bad when I think it was the angel of the Lord who needed to intervene on the donkey's behalf. Because of Balaam's anger, the Lord opened the donkey's mouth! She was a good donkey to him all his days.

A Believing Believer

As Christians, we were given the gifts, talents, and abilities to speak and spread praise, worship, and work toward the salvation of others, but there are times when we disobey the Lord. With our disobedience, sometimes the Lord reverted to the animals to do his bidding! Those blessed animals listen and obey his voice. I believe that is why the animals will also be blessed beyond measure, perhaps leading to the spirits of our pets and animals coming into the kingdom!

Praise will not only come from creatures great and small but also all heaven, earth, sun, moon, and every star in the galaxy, that every raindrop might chime and every wind might whistle along with the coolness of the dew. From this symphony, all heaven and earth will sing or play some instruments to the new creation. I believe even the animals will have their place accordingly for more than any imagination can perceive, and all for God's glory.

I can only imagine birds singing, crickets chirping, dogs howling, frogs croaking, cats meowing, harps playing, lions roaring, and everything of God's creation. Not to mention angels with harps and horns—music just from their wings and dewdrops become drumbeats upon a single leaf. Imagine: Scripture says no eye has seen or ear heard what is ours to behold when the day of our arrival and destination comes. Our future home surpasses any human understanding. We do not know what awaits us in heaven.

> But as it is written, Eye hath not seen, nor ear heard, neither have entered into the heart of man, the things which God hath prepared for them that love him. (1 Corinthians 2:9)

We can only imagine how wonderful the garden of Eden was, and now we can only imagine how wonderful the final heaven will be.

Mother Teresa is quoted as saying, "They [animals] too, are created by the same loving hand of God which created us... It is our duty to protect them and to promote their well-being." We owe it to them, as they serve us with docility and loyalty. The continuation of the love of God keeps showing through His creatures and His creations.

Eternal Love

The enduring love of God to not only give humans another chance for a new place in heaven, but also that there might be a provision for our pets, is amazing! Pets in our care show separation anxiety as humans do. Because the animals were also separated in Eden from a merciful God, I believe in the restoration of animals into a new heaven and a new earth. We are redeemed through Christ.

The shadows of sin are here, like in Noah's day. There was separation then, but along with this story, Noah and his family and the animals were saved, restored, and given another chance at eternal life through faith, trust, belief, and repentance. The Lord found favor with Noah and his family, along with the whole ark. This gives me another reason to believe.

God is even making a covenant to animals:

> And God spake unto Noah, and to his sons with him, saying, And I, behold, I establish my covenant with you, and with your seed after you; And with every living creature that is with you, of the fowl, of the cattle, and of every beast of the earth with you; from all that go out of the ark, to every beast of the earth. (Genesis 9:8–10)

> Bring forth with thee every living thing that is with thee, of all flesh, both of fowl, and of cattle, and of every creeping thing that creepeth upon the earth; that they may breed abundantly in the earth, and be fruitful, and multiply upon the earth. (Genesis 8:17)

It's hard to fathom creeping things on God's love list, but there it is, making a covenant to save them (even though I think they are unlovable).

From Eden to Eternity

How can we imagine heaven? Will we know all that went before us? I believe so. Without a doubt, the Creator of all the world created everything with a DNA file in every living, breathing thing! Not only will we have identification, but even a new name just for each and every one. It is certainly not to keep tabs on us but for the mysteries of things unknown and yet to come! The world is in a survival mode for existence, but I marvel at the instincts of all creatures and animals. One of my favorites is when a robin will put his ear to the ground to hear a worm so as to feed her nest of baby birds! Creatures were given the ability to survive due to the fall of man, but the love of God has every feather counted!

What sound does a worm make?

Dog Gone

In all my years as a dog breeder, I've witnessed the very depths of joy and the very crushing pain of loss. In my belief, there seems to be a special place for pets with God, and He has made a plan for animals in heaven, especially as thoughtfully revealed to us through the characteristics of love and loyalty our pets show toward us. No other animal shows just how much it wants to make us happy. Nothing else can reverse our mood, attitude, depression, sorrow, and tears. Even in happiness, they make us happier, making us laugh and smile. They seem to be the only ones able to do this. Their tails tell us much about how they try to interact and how much they are with us in our silence. The people in our lives use the tongue. In many cases, wrong words are said for comfort, which can lead to misunderstandings and sometimes arguments.

In those moments of silence when our pets appear, I would love to fully understand the ability they have as a comforter! There is a deep thought pattern we will not understand! Why do we hurt so much when the pet we love dies? Like in marriage, there becomes a bond that death breaks. The very pain and separation are a part of the process we have to endure. This started because of the sin in the beginning, yet I believe the joy will reveal itself once again in eternal bliss. We get a taste of this weather followed by the rainbow bridge our pets cross, or after death stings like a storm in our hearts, we see a new rainbow of promise for eternity. In eternal love, I believe we will all meet our Maker, the Creator, Savior, and Lord of all. All the pain in life will be gone and will not be remembered or, on any level, endured anymore. All in the glory of Jesus.

This is such a doggone thing to endure, but the Bible teaches us that it is only for a time.

Oops, Wrong Direction

And the same John had his raiment of camel's
hair, and a leathern girdle about his loins; and his
meat was locusts and wild honey. (Matthew 3:4)

Surely, the camel's hair was a needed thing, along with the locusts
and wild honey, for survival. The Lord had his eye on John and his
trip, but John traveled as any poor man could!

Scripture talks about the camel's hair on a poor man, then about
a camel compared to a rich man. Camels have a priority position, as
seen in this scripture: "Then said Jesus unto his disciples, Verily I
say unto you, That a rich man shall hardly enter into the kingdom
of heaven" (Matthew 19:23). A rich man shall hardly enter into the
(right direction) kingdom of heaven, for the scripture says that it is
easier for a camel to go through the eye of a needle than for a rich
man to enter into the kingdom of God.

A point to consider is the value of the Lord using a camel,
considering the camel leading the direction of the wise men into
Bethlehem in the direction of a star. This unfolds how the Lord used
not just men of the Bible but the use of camels for the direction—
the right direction—to Christ, our Lord. From the raiment of the
camel's hair for the survival journey to passing through the eye of the
needle into survival and into the direction of the kingdom of God for
the ultimate survival. Even the camels will have their story to share
upon entering the gates. The journey has led many to Christ by the
star and camel into Bethlehem! Out of the eye of the needle, into the
direction of Jesus of Bethlehem!

Connecting the Dots

Bird Tweets

Birds of a feather flock together, not only for the guidance of a flock leader but I think also for little chat. This relationship of tweeting and tattling among themselves is great, but not just among themselves, as seen in the following scripture:

> And it shall be, that thou shalt drink of the
> brook; and I have commanded the ravens to
> feed thee there...And the ravens brought him
> bread and flesh in the morning, and bread and
> flesh in the evening; and he drank of the brook.
> (1 Kings 17:4, 6)

This was done for Elijah, the prophet, for three and a half years!

> A righteous man regardeth the life of his beast:
> but the tender mercies of the wicked are cruel.
> (Proverbs 12:10)

Filling in the gap and between the lines of my mind's writing on the wall, I perceive the instruction of ravens bringing meals only two times a day: morning and evening. So why do I indulge in more than that sometimes! Satisfaction with only two meals a day will give a better figure! Meat, bread, and bottled brook water—satisfaction guaranteed!

Saintly Angels

A righteous man regardeth the life of his beast:
but the tender mercies of the wicked are cruel.
(Proverbs 12:10)

So shall it be in heaven. Believing Christians have the authority to call themselves saints. But there are also angels on earth among us. Sometimes, I wish to have the given authority from God to claim myself as an angel instead of a saint on earth. I could do needed things invisibly, unseen, and still proclaim the Gospel!

But the Lord loves His saints:

> For the Lord loveth judgment, and forsaketh not his saints; they are preserved for ever: but the seed of the wicked shall be cut off. The righteous shall inherit the land, and dwell therein for ever. (Psalm 37:28–29)

If given the opportunity to live a little longer, it would allow me to acknowledge the miracles in life and cover the shadows of any doubt! May God's grace and mercy serve your direction with God's providential love and care.

Human Pencil

This human pencil is not always sharp at the point, but animals have a lot to say in the Bible. Whether talking, crying, or groaning, the animals brought the point to be said! If only we humans groaned a little louder than animals, "because the creature itself also shall be delivered from the bondage of corruption into the glorious liberty of the children of God" (Romans 8:21). Have I mentioned that animals and pets will be in heaven? I believe they are and have suffered through no fault of their own.

> How do the beasts groan! The herds of cattle are perplexed, because they have no pasture; yea, the flocks of sheep are made desolate. O Lord, to thee will I cry: for the fire hath devoured the pastures of the wilderness, and the flame hath burned all the trees of the field. The beasts of the field cry also unto thee: for the rivers of waters are dried up, and the fire hath devoured the pastures of the wilderness. (Joel 1:18–20)

The beasts cry. Why? We have made the animals suffer from the consequences of our sin on this earth. How thankful we are that Jesus has made all things right! May God be glorified by all mankind, animals, and plants.

No End in Sight

Comprehension of a life with no end is too much for me to comprehend, like the endless galaxy! I always have a need to end my workday or a project to be finished. I myself like to end my day, be on schedule, plan ahead, say no, cover my head, and go back to sleep. What is it going to be like with endless rest? No pain anywhere with a beautiful body. No irritations over daily problems. No anxieties over earthly life. No stress over death. I can't imagine not having a mind for troubling things or the earthy work presented for more than seventy years. Everything will be eternal for all eternity! Getting bored is my nature. How will I cope with that? I trust that has all been figured out by God, as He says He has prepared a place for me with a new name, and I will never have to set a timer! God has a plan unspeakably unimaginable, and so will let my excitement build while I wait for that glorious day! Seeing all my friends and family I've known throughout the years will be wonderful in itself. Just a visit to each person would not fill eternity but certainly can pass a lot of time! The joy of reuniting will be on my list of things to do! Of course, after I visit my heavenly Father first!

Tattle Tails

It has been fun and adventurous for me to be able to share scriptures and thoughts on animals and heavenly things! When we think of animals, pets, and the souls of humans, the souls of animals come to my mind.

> But ask now the beasts, and they shall teach thee;
> and the fowls of the air, and they shall tell thee:
> Or speak to the earth, and it shall teach thee:
> and the fishes of the sea shall declare unto thee.
> Who knoweth not in all these that the hand of
> the Lord hath wrought this? In whose hand is the
> soul of every living thing, and the breath of all
> mankind. (Job 12:7–10)

We are in His hands, humans and pets: "Thy righteousness is like the great mountains; thy judgments are a great deep: O Lord, thou preservest man and beast" (Psalm 36:6).

Provoking Thought to the Final Conclusion

My wish for *Tattle Tails* is that it will give some soulful food to some readers on behalf of all living and breathing beings, to give you some peace to help you in some way. This is not very detailed, but it may be enough to put your mind in a positive direction and maybe enough to provoke some of your own investigation into the truth of the Scripture. Maybe to bring you into some thoughts about what needs to be revealed about you—thoughts about how to see the future of your loved ones and your loyal pets and the world of animals. I've mentioned the end, but the beginning starts with the realization of who holds the air we breathe to the end. God's providence will lead us to the end!

> Then shall the dust return to the earth as it was: and the spirit shall return unto God who gave it. (Ecclesiastes 12:7)

> And moreover, because the preacher was wise, he still taught the people knowledge; yea, he gave good heed, and sought out, and set in order many proverbs. (Ecclesiastes 12:9)

> Let us hear the conclusion of the whole matter: Fear God, and keep his commandments: for this is the whole duty of man. (Ecclesiastes 12:13)

For God shall bring every work into judgment, with every secret thing, whether it be good or whether it be evil. If my time continues into more days, I would like to take on the challenge of writing another book on why I believe I am one of God's faithful servants through all the miracles and providence of God and what He has sent my way for these earthly challenges for seventy-plus years, and the destiny of it all.

Did I Say *the End*?

It has come to my attention that I need an end, but I can't find an end! In heaven, there is no end! While I try to find an end, I find the end of myself. I get lost in my mind when I think God hasn't come to His end.

> And if I go and prepare a place for you, I will come again, and receive you unto myself; that where I am, there ye may be also. (John 14:3)

So far and for so long, He must still be getting ready for us. It took Noah 120 years to build the ark under specific instructions with just Noah's family! God has spent hundreds of years preparing for us, and when done, God's plan is to come get those waiting for the return to come, for those waiting for the finale finally! No wonder it's taking so long. Heaven will be endless!

Desire

Holy Father, make me into the image of your son, Jesus Christ.
That I may live a full life of love, patience, and humility.
Let my love shine forth unto others, so thy grace
will awaken your sleeping children.
I yield to your desire, to restore souls who are lost.
Hear my prayer, Lord. Take my hand and walk us to salvation.
So we may come to share in the glory of God.

CPSIA information can be obtained
at www.ICGtesting.com
Printed in the USA
BVHW041108040523
663580BV00005B/257

9 798887 632261